I0502462

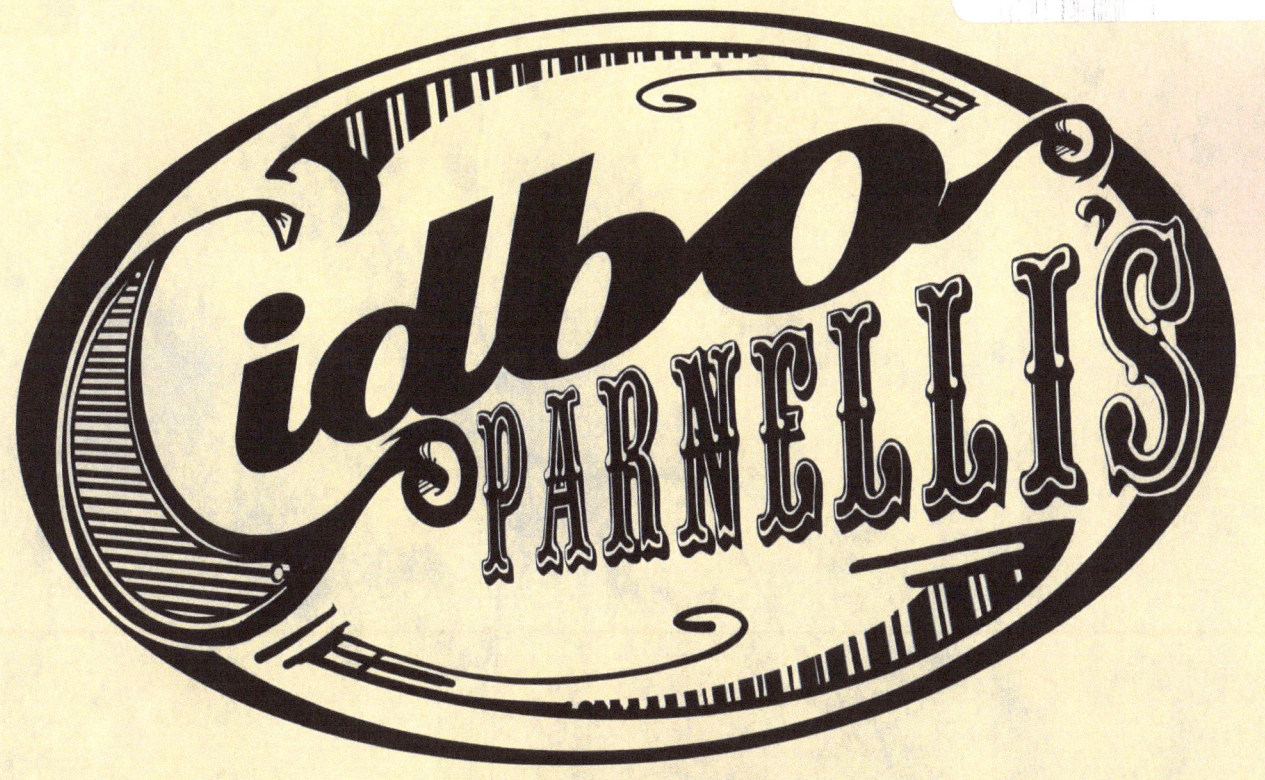

JOSCH EDGINGTON
WENDI EDGINGTON
KEL LOUDERBACK
JUSTIN AUTREY

PRINTED BY CREATESPACE AN AMAZON COMPANY

CONTENTS ARE PROPERTY OF KEL LOUDERBACK, JOSH EDGINGTON,
WENDI EDGINGTON AND JUSTIN AUTREY
ANY REPRODUCTION WITHOUT PRIOR WRITTEN CONSENT
IS STRONGLY PROHIBITED BY LAW

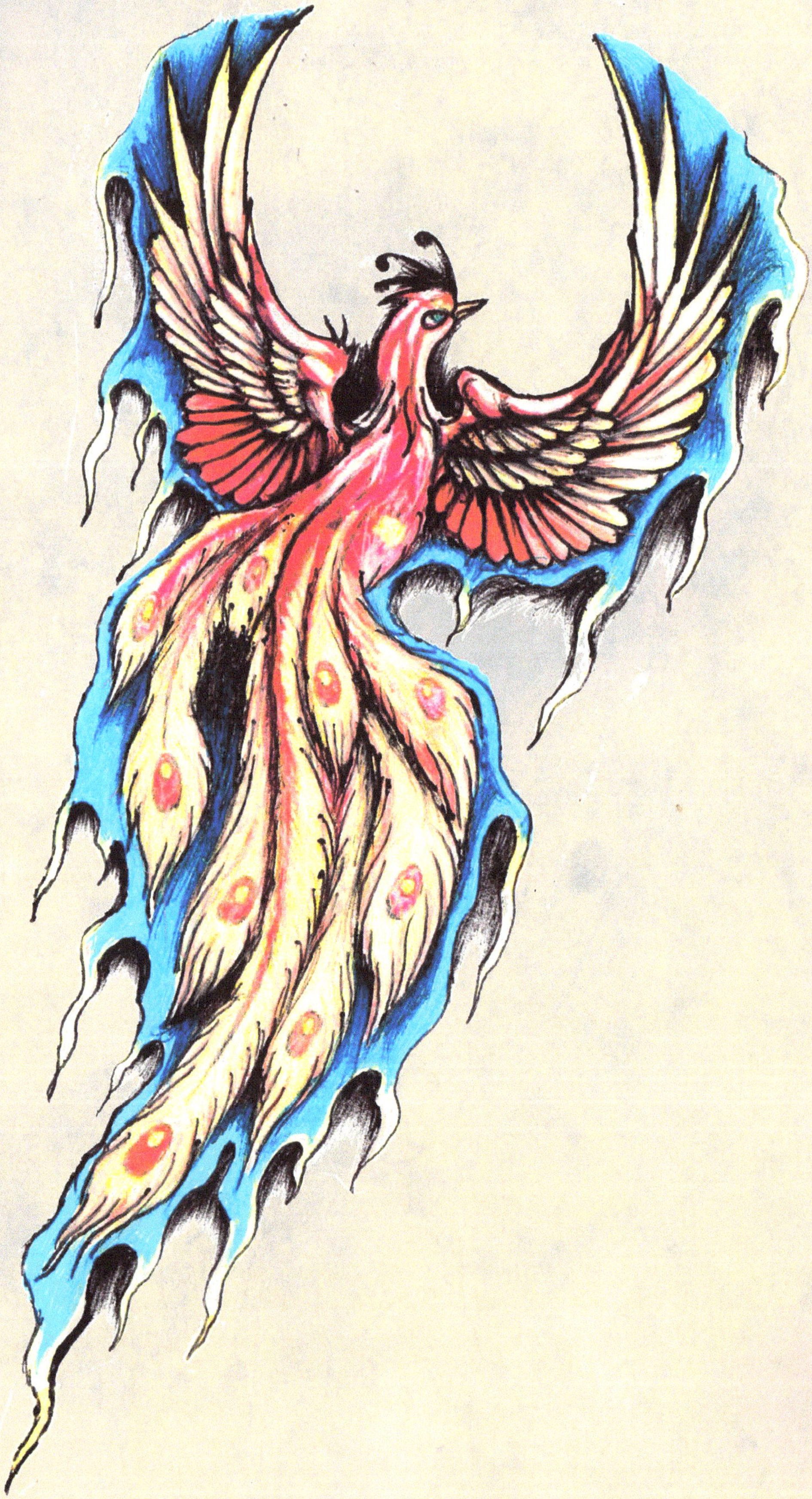

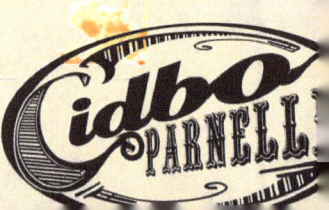

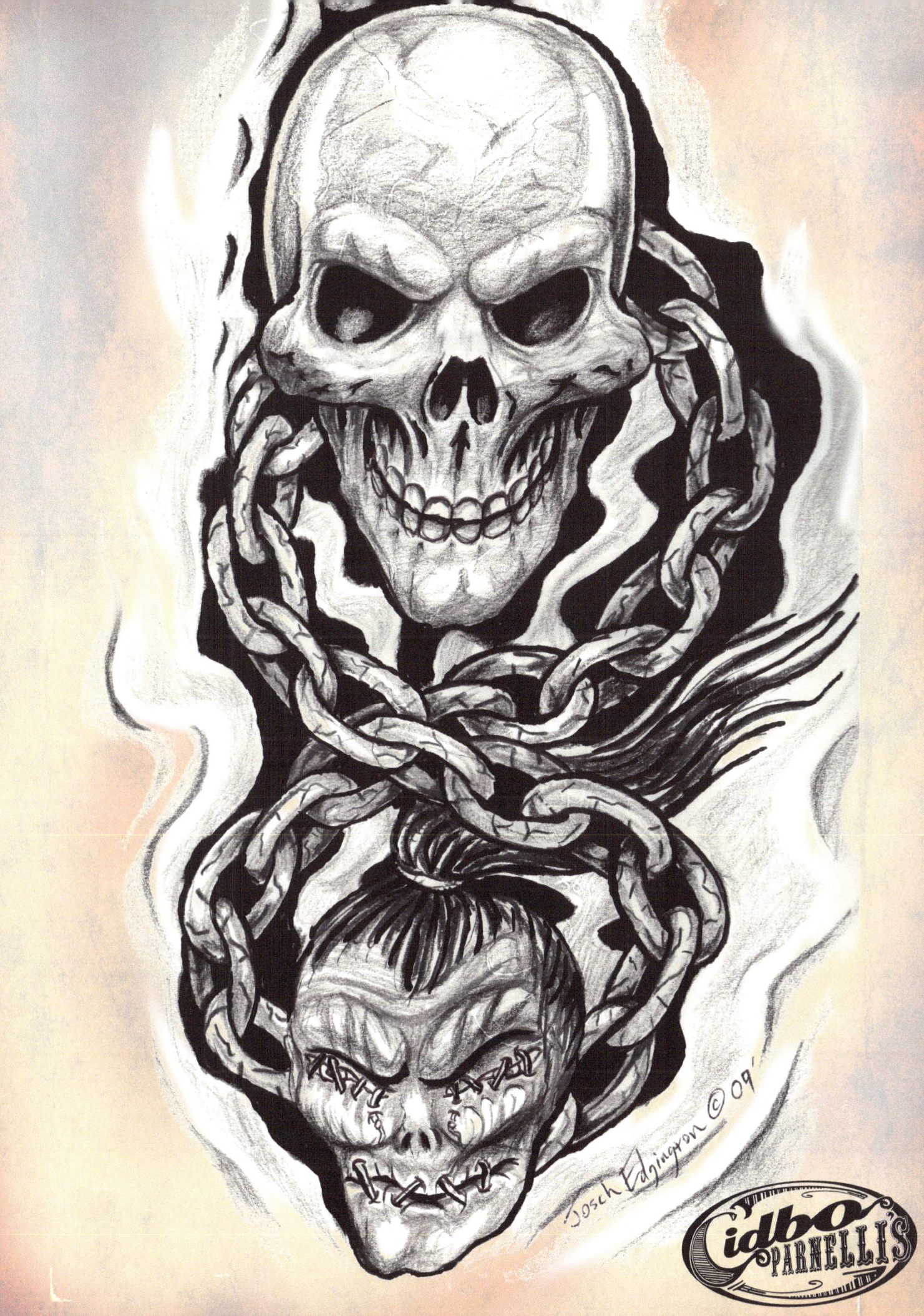

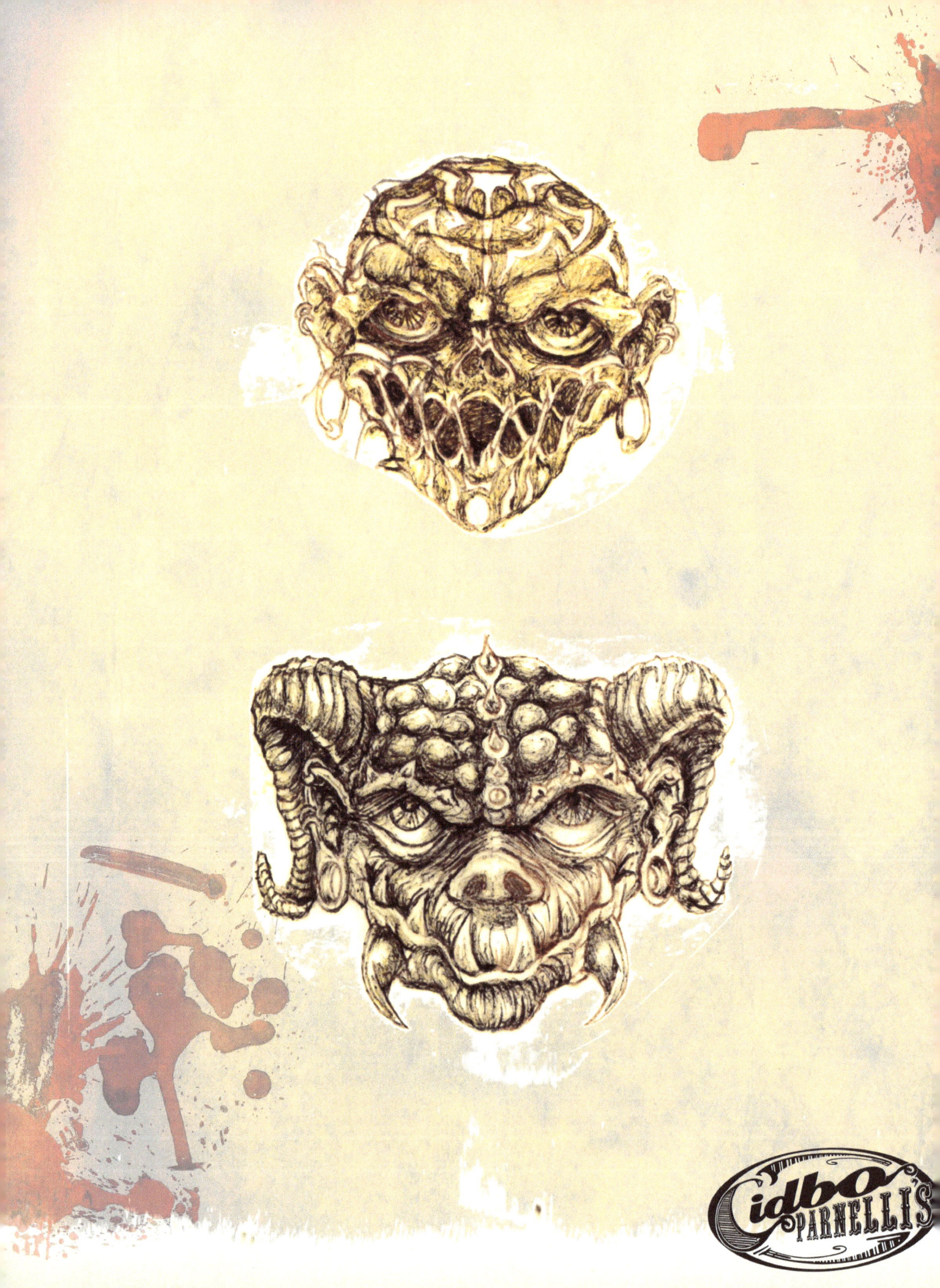

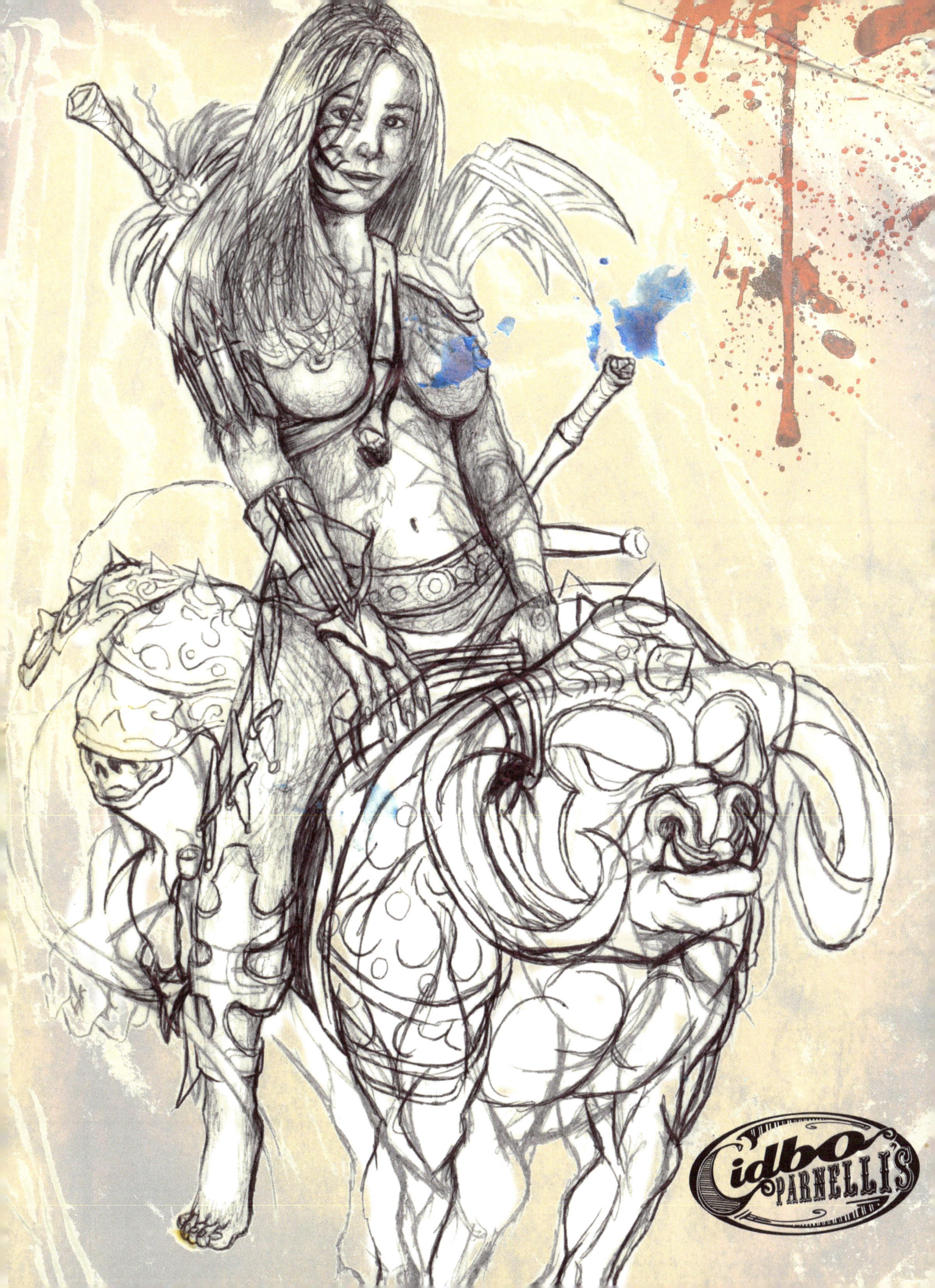

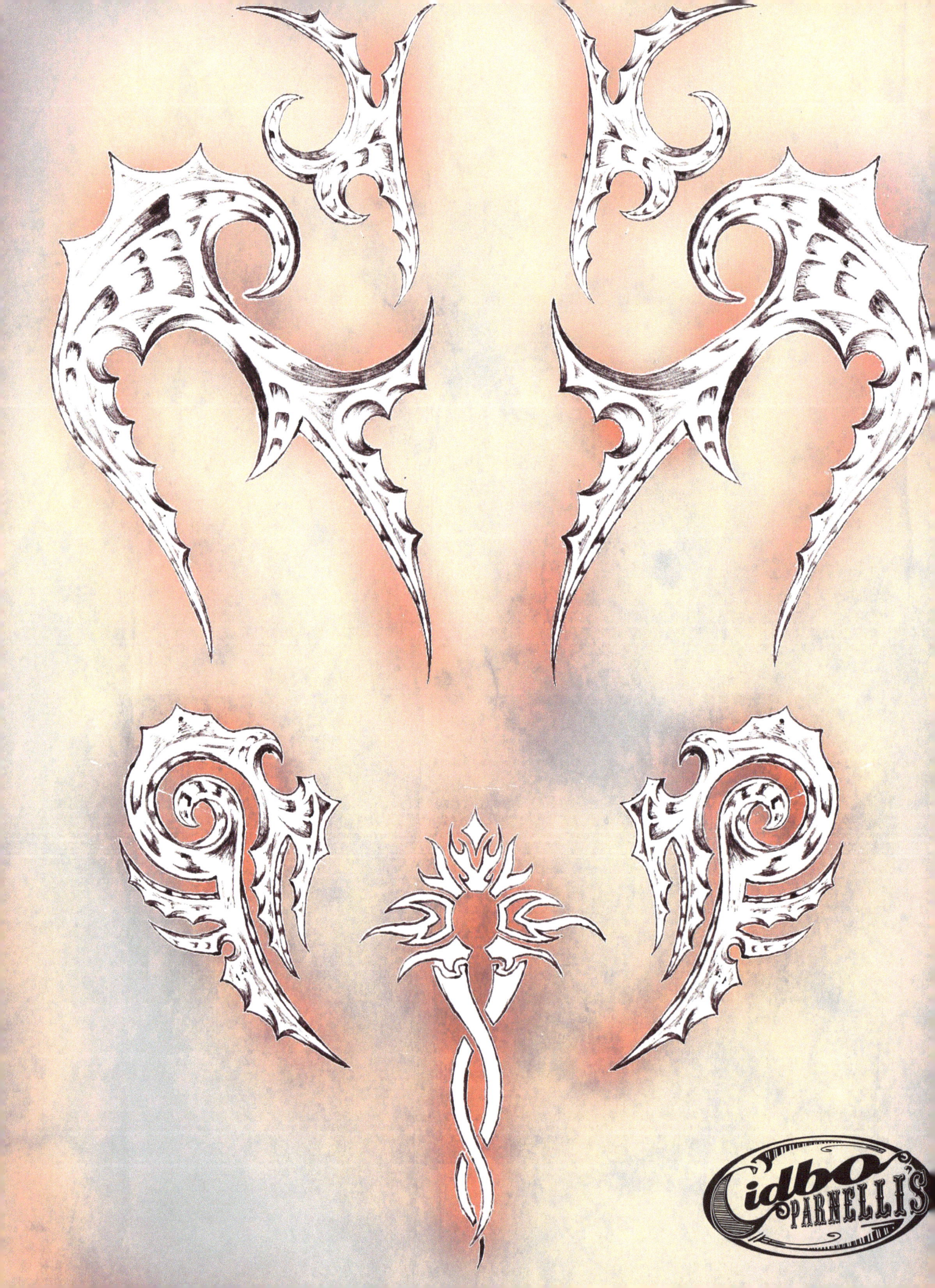

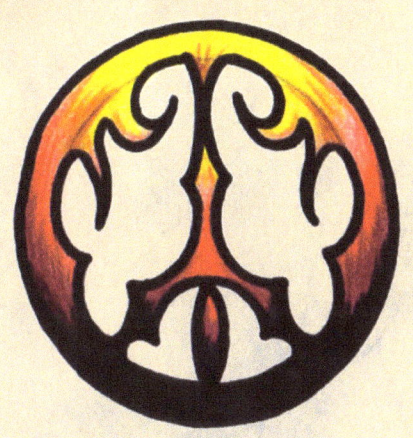
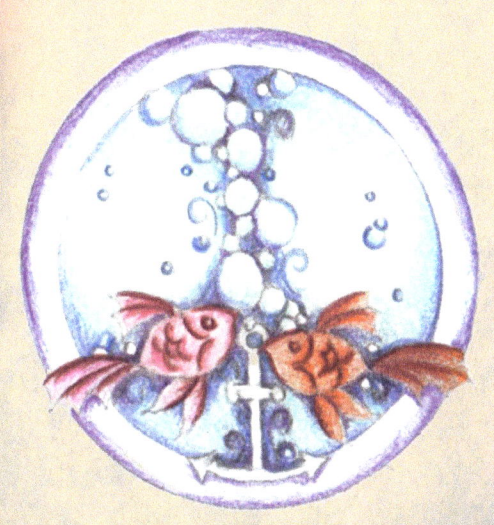
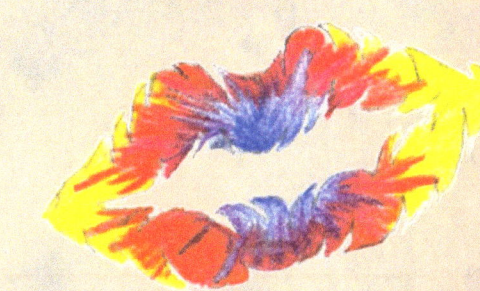
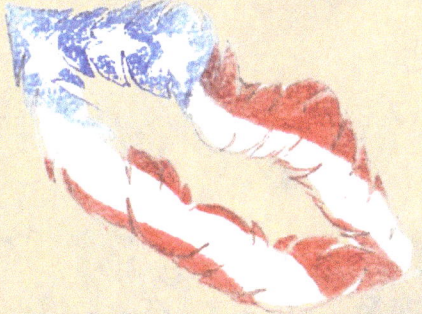
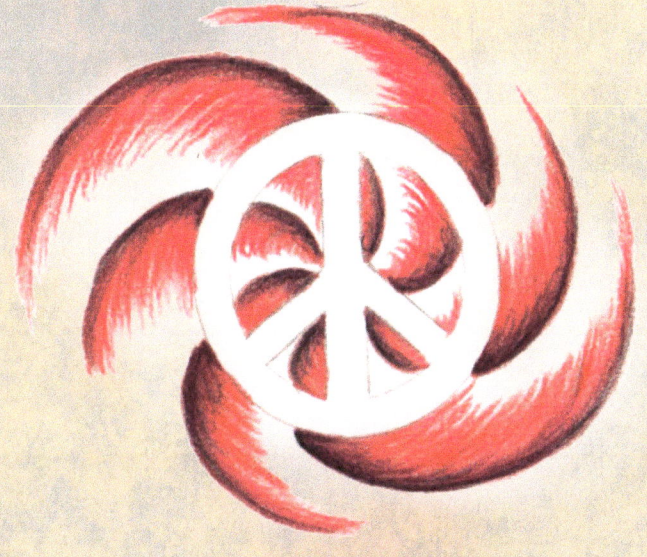
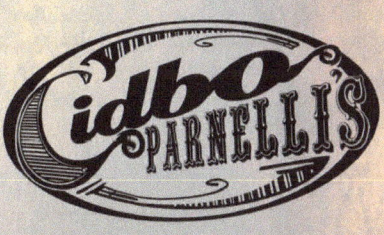

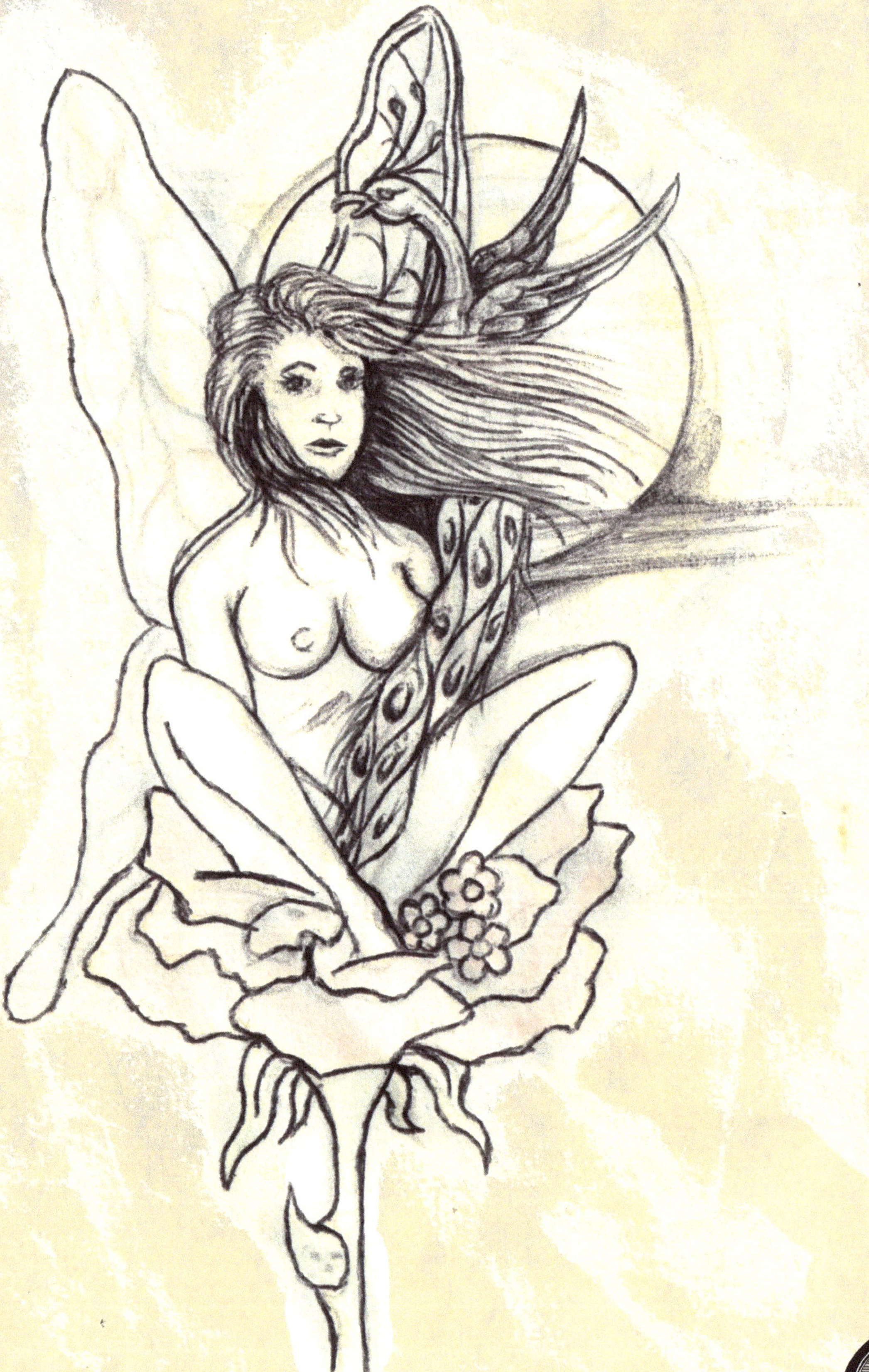

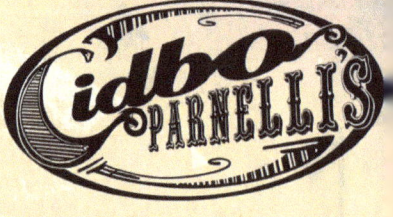

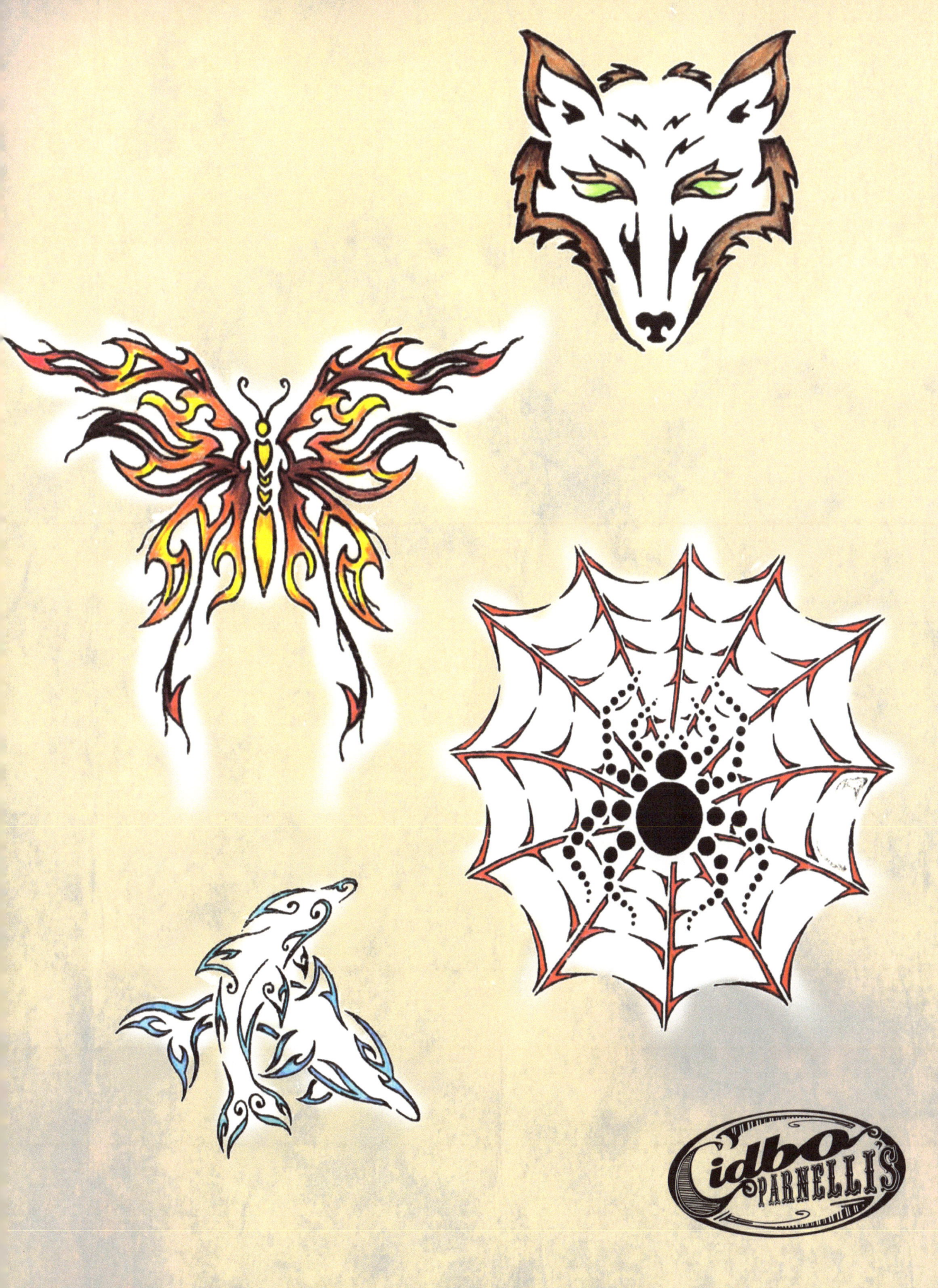

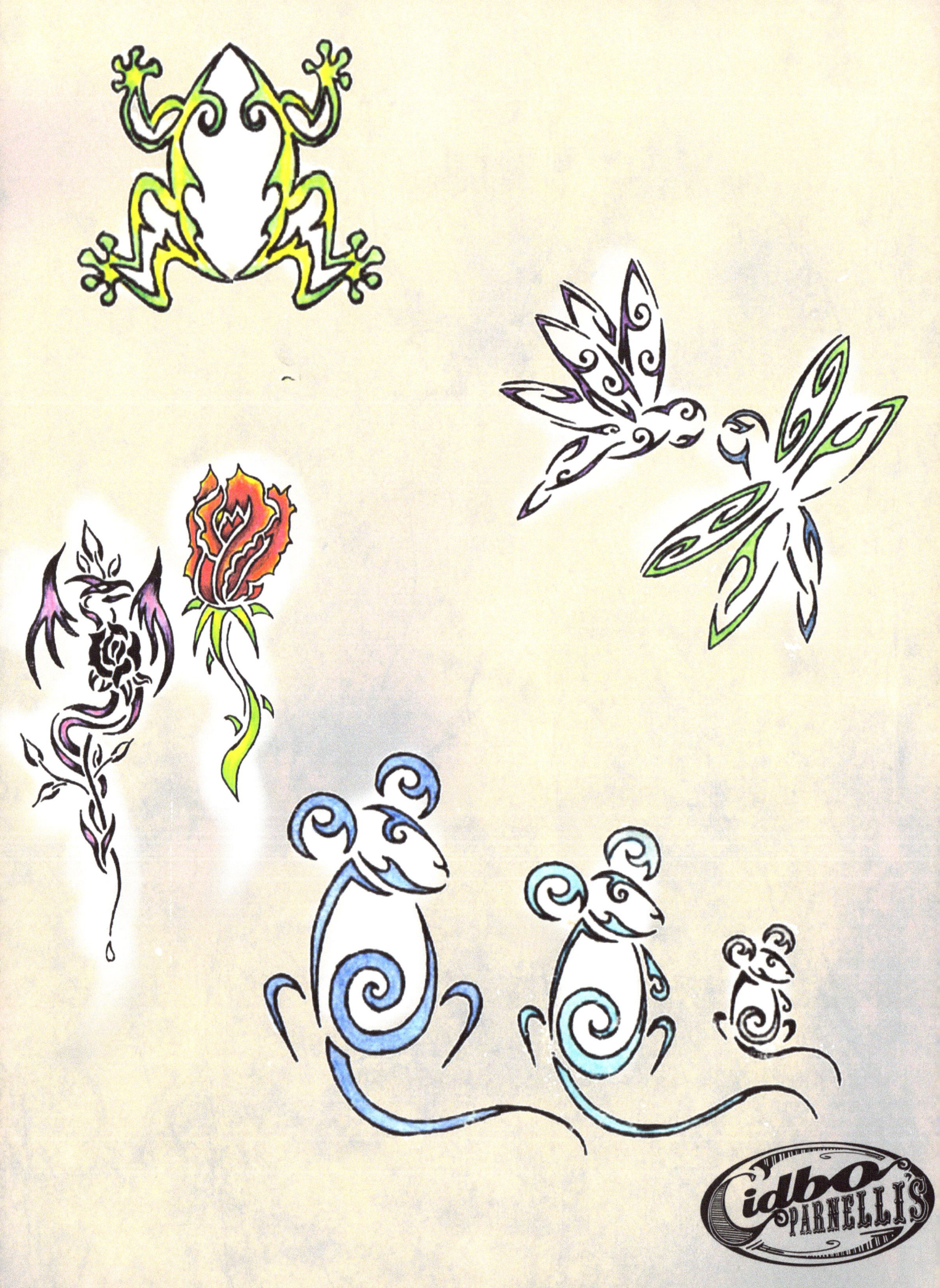

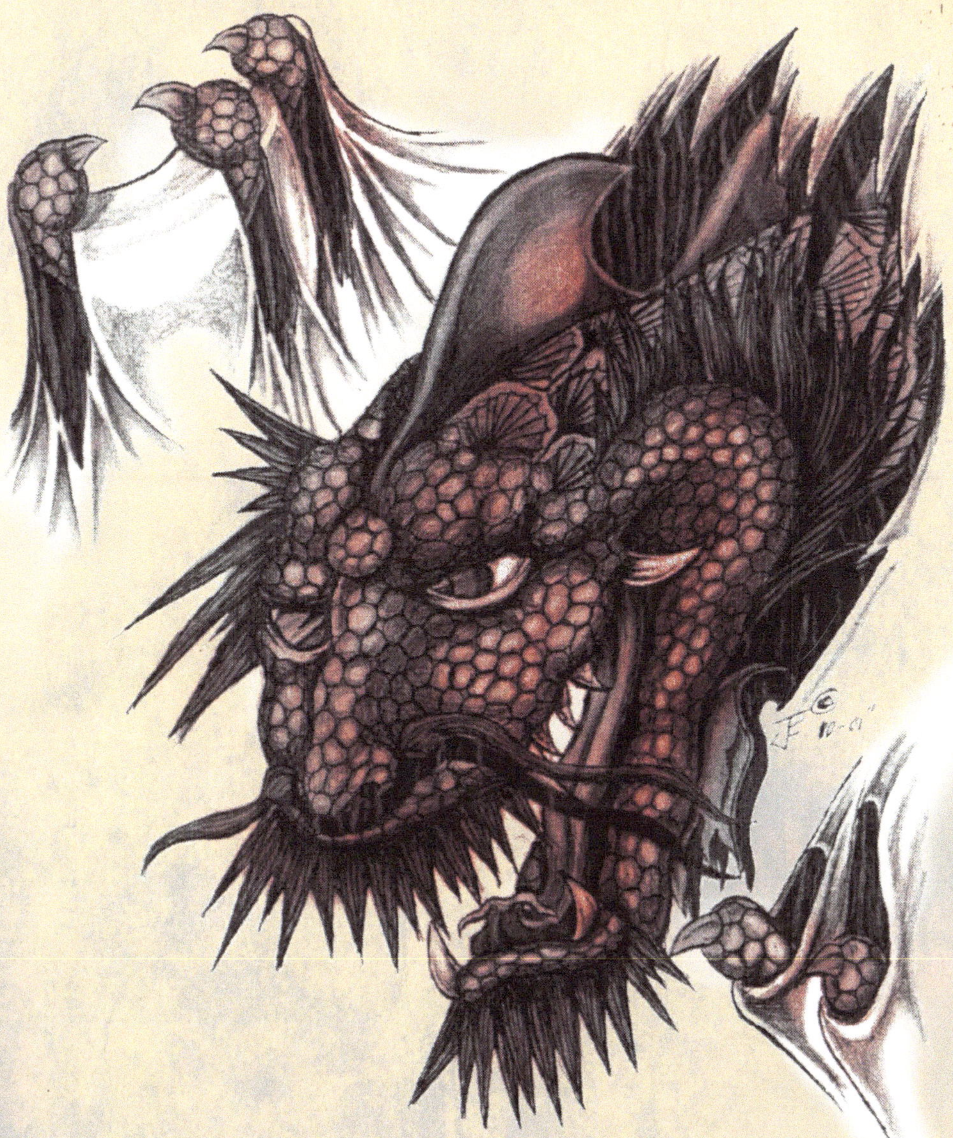

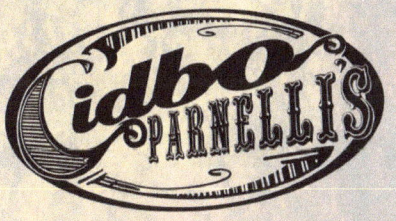

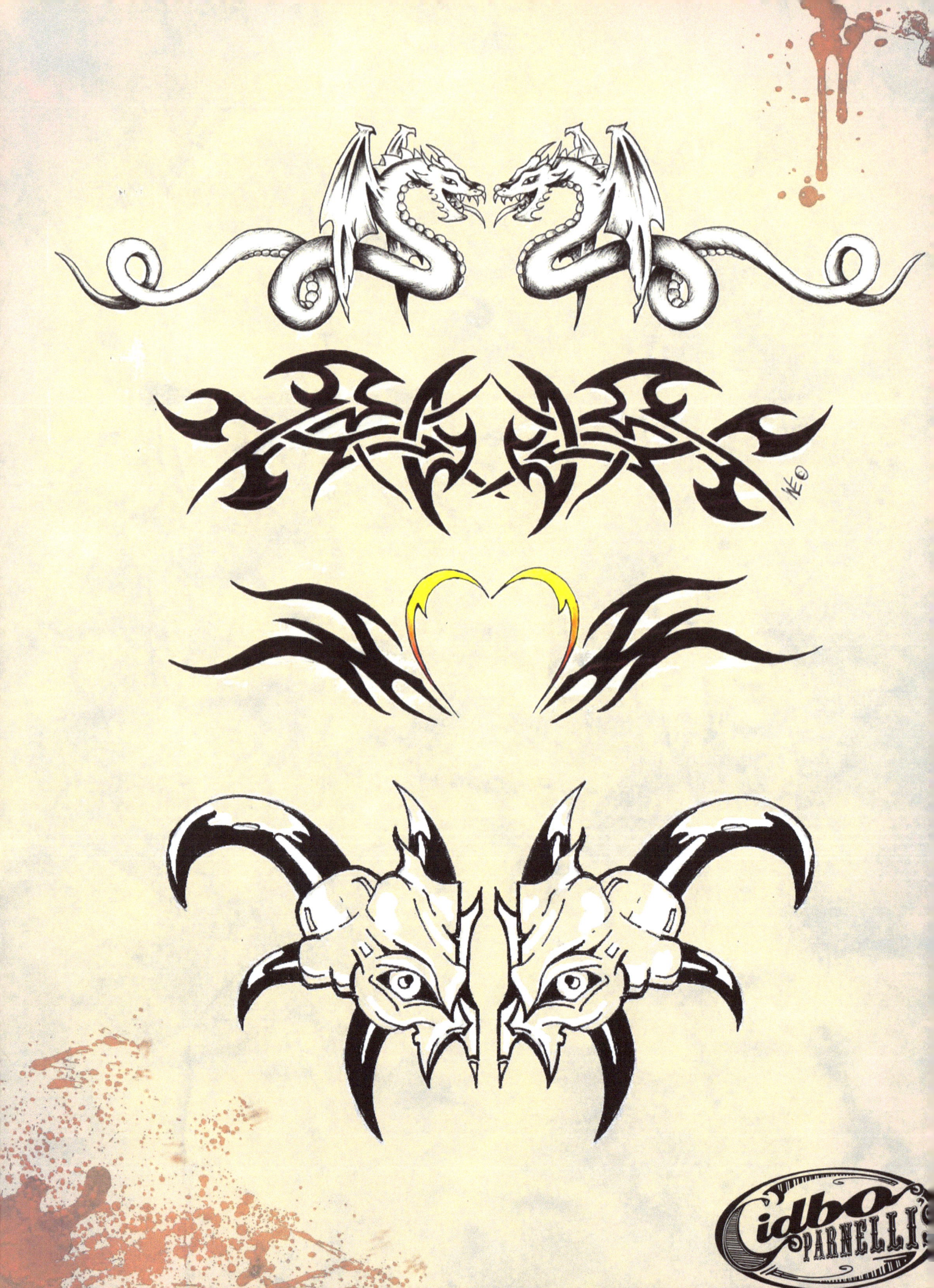

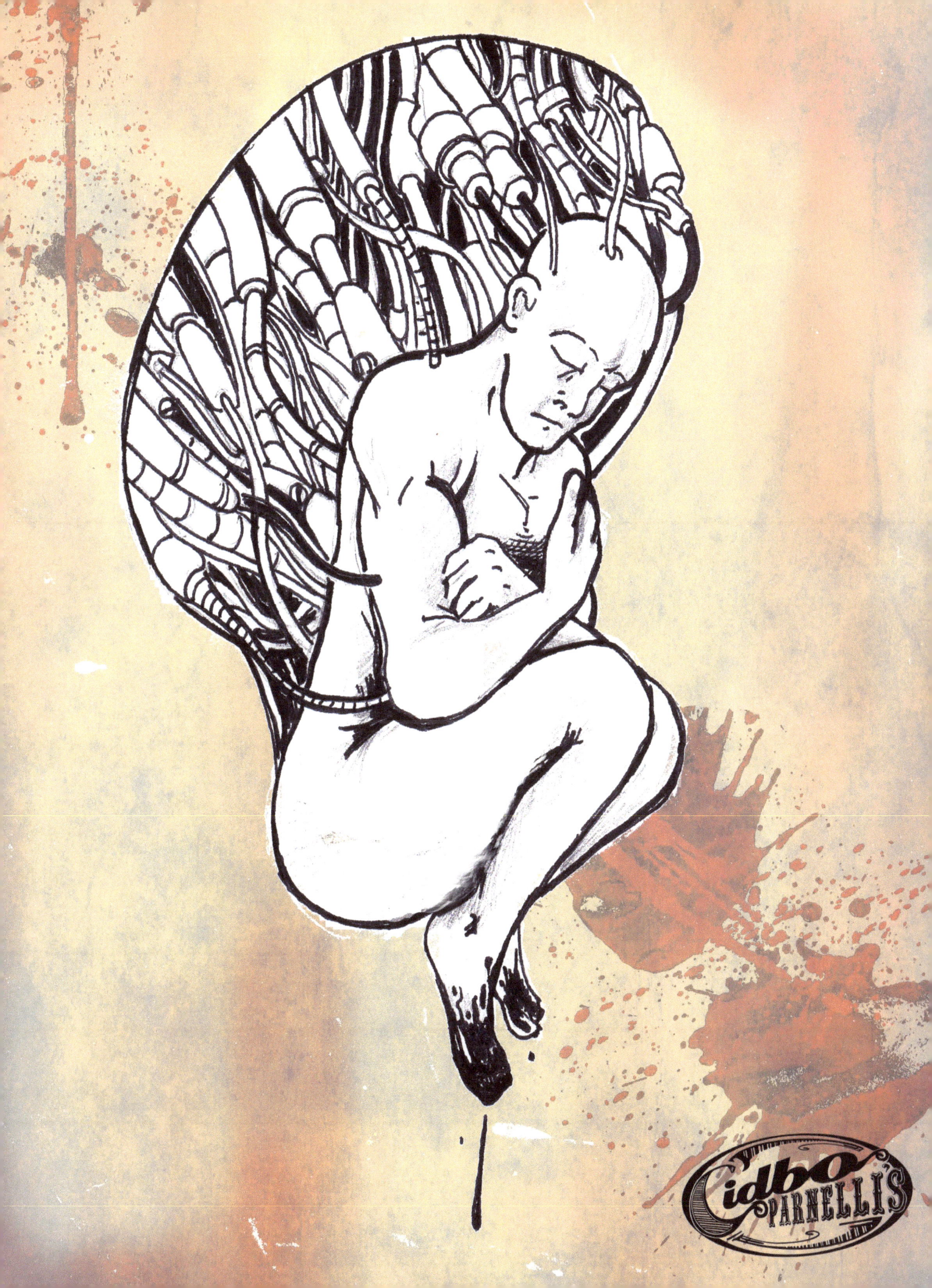

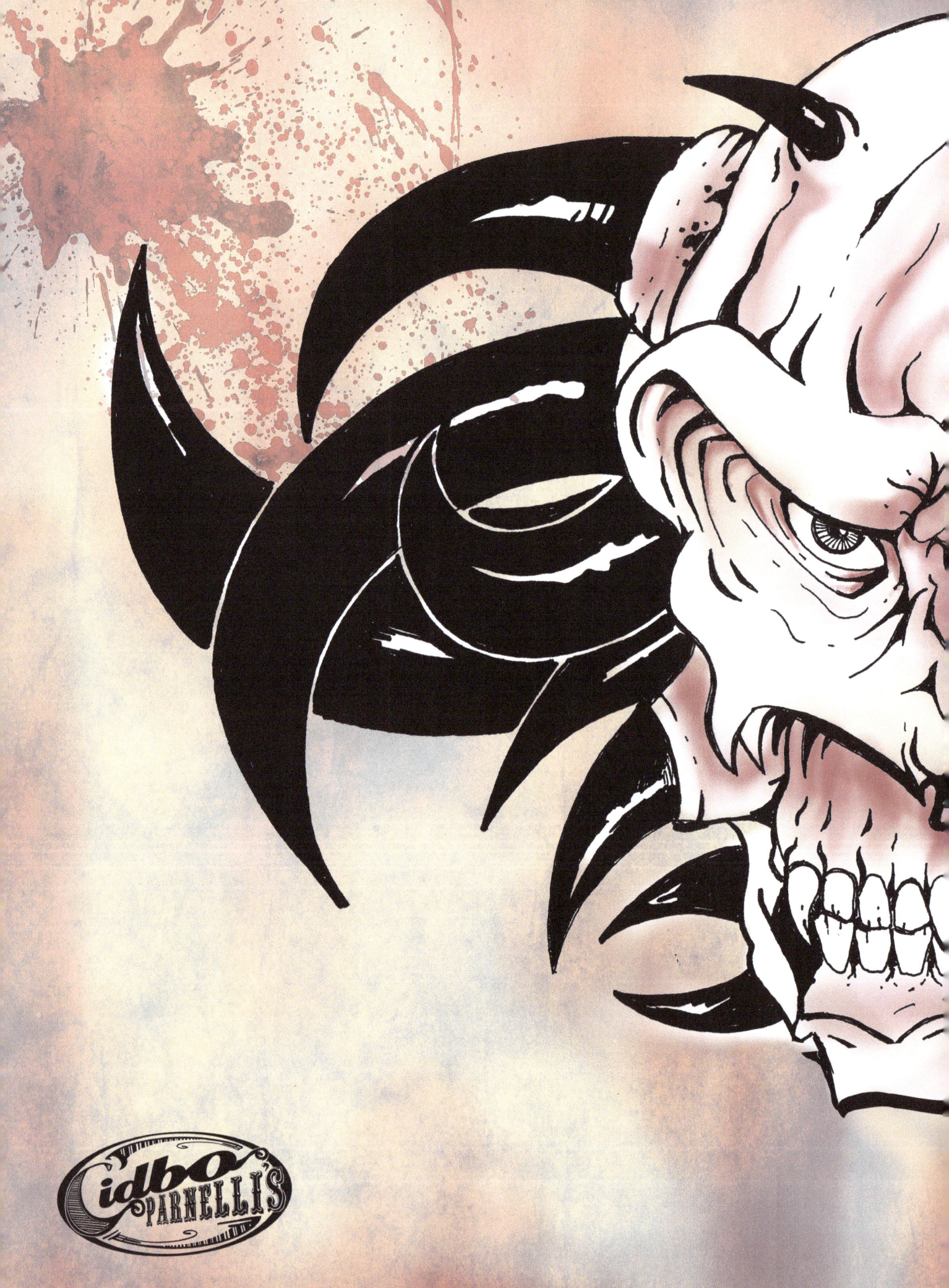

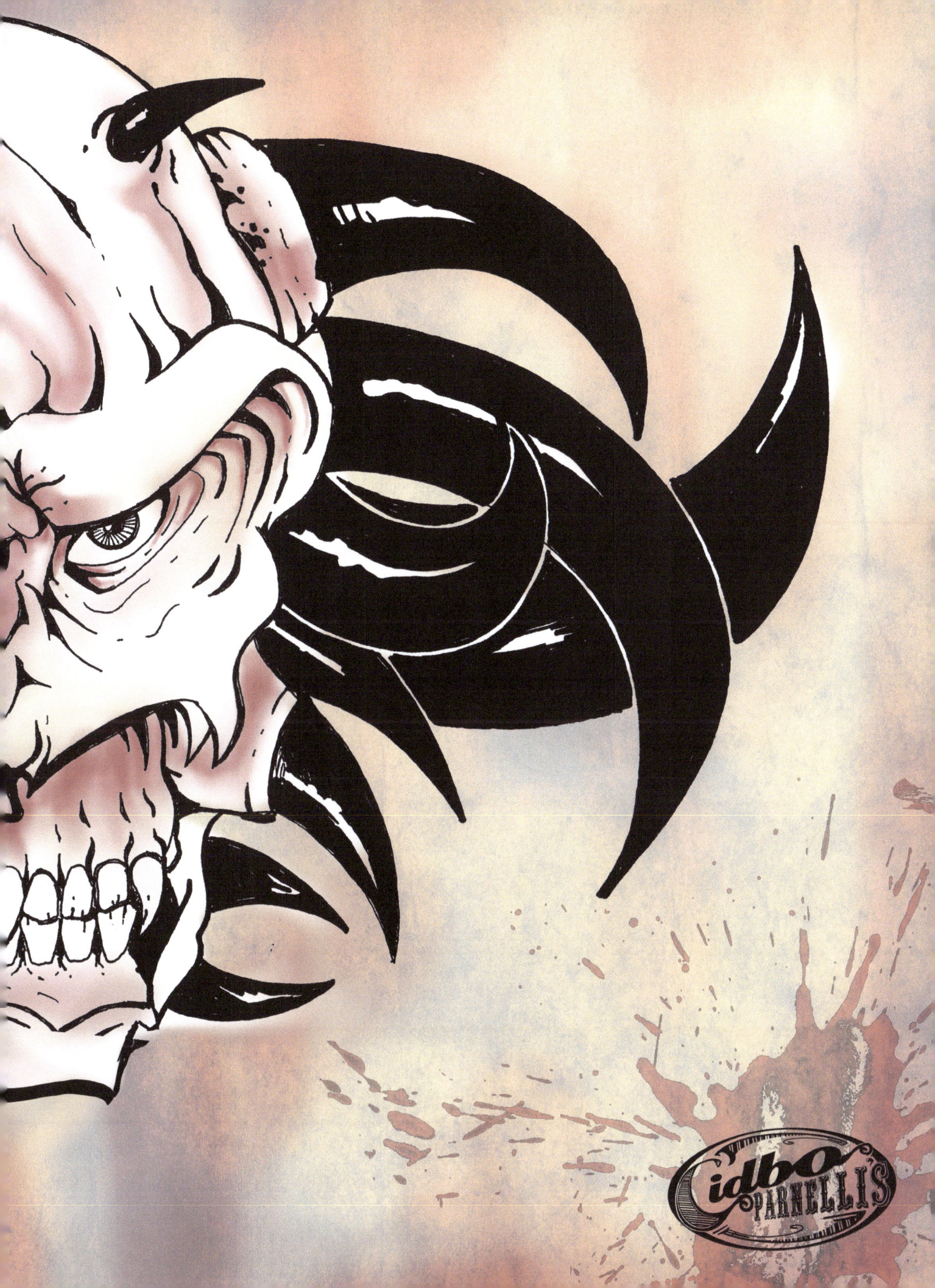

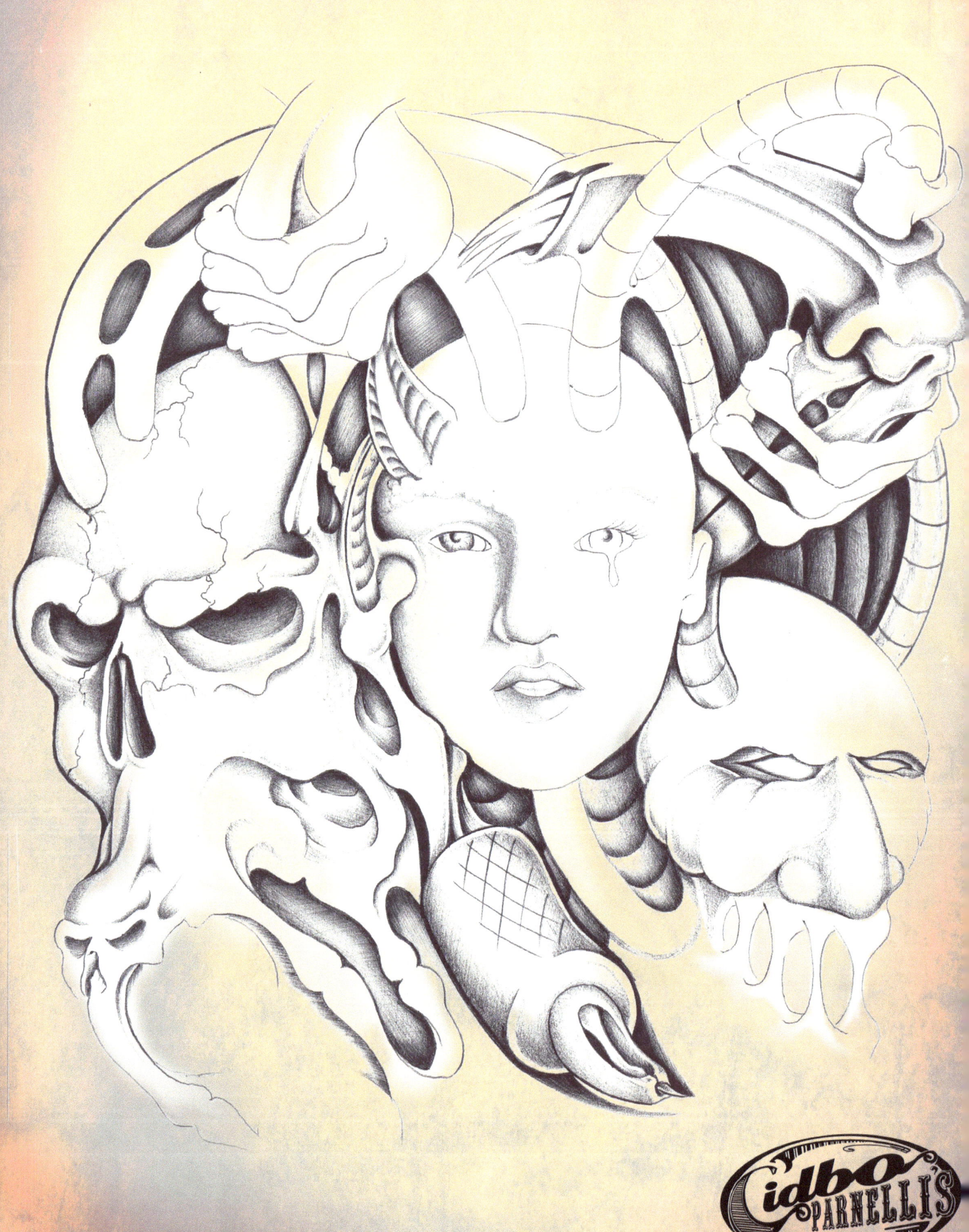

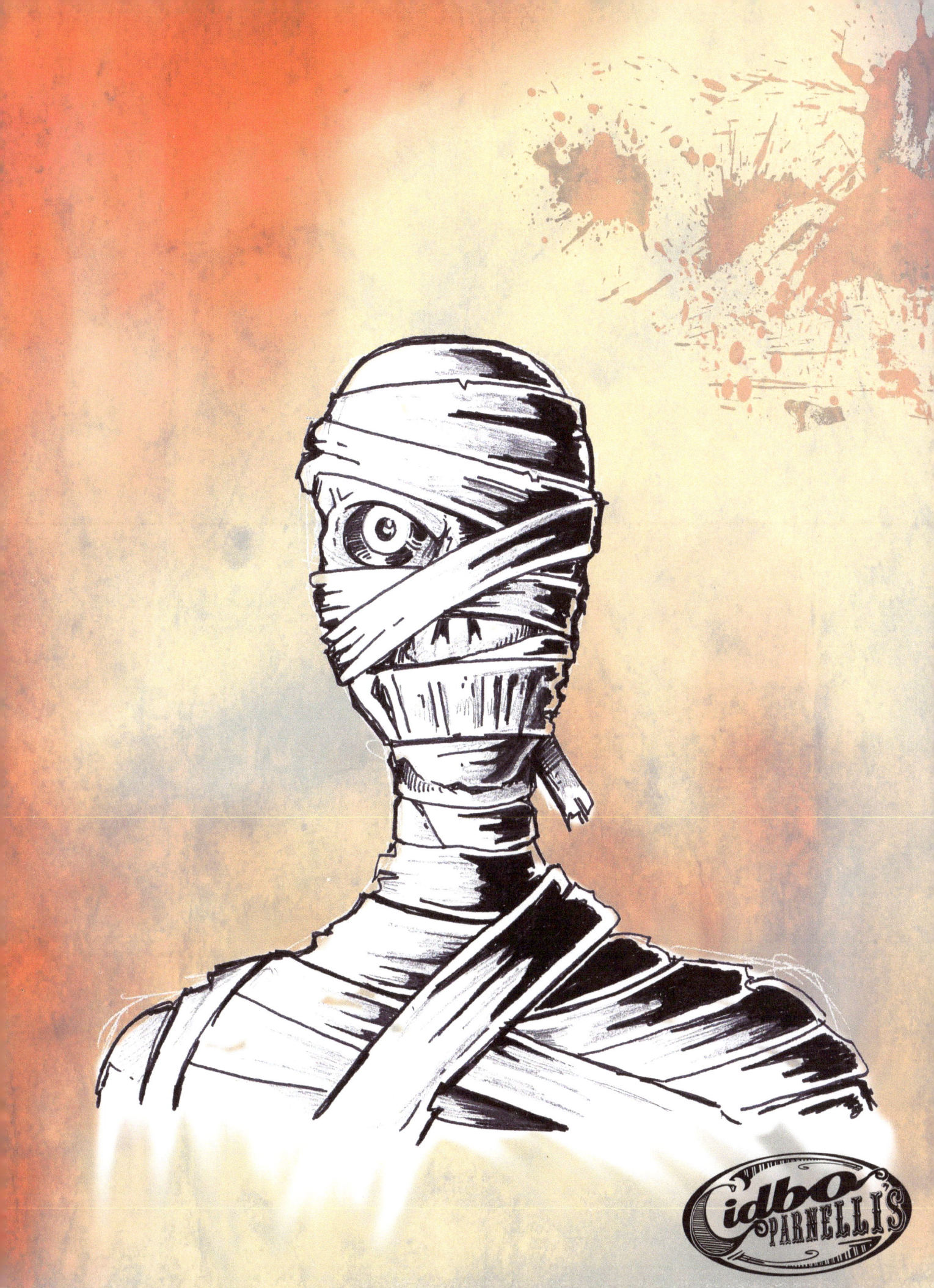

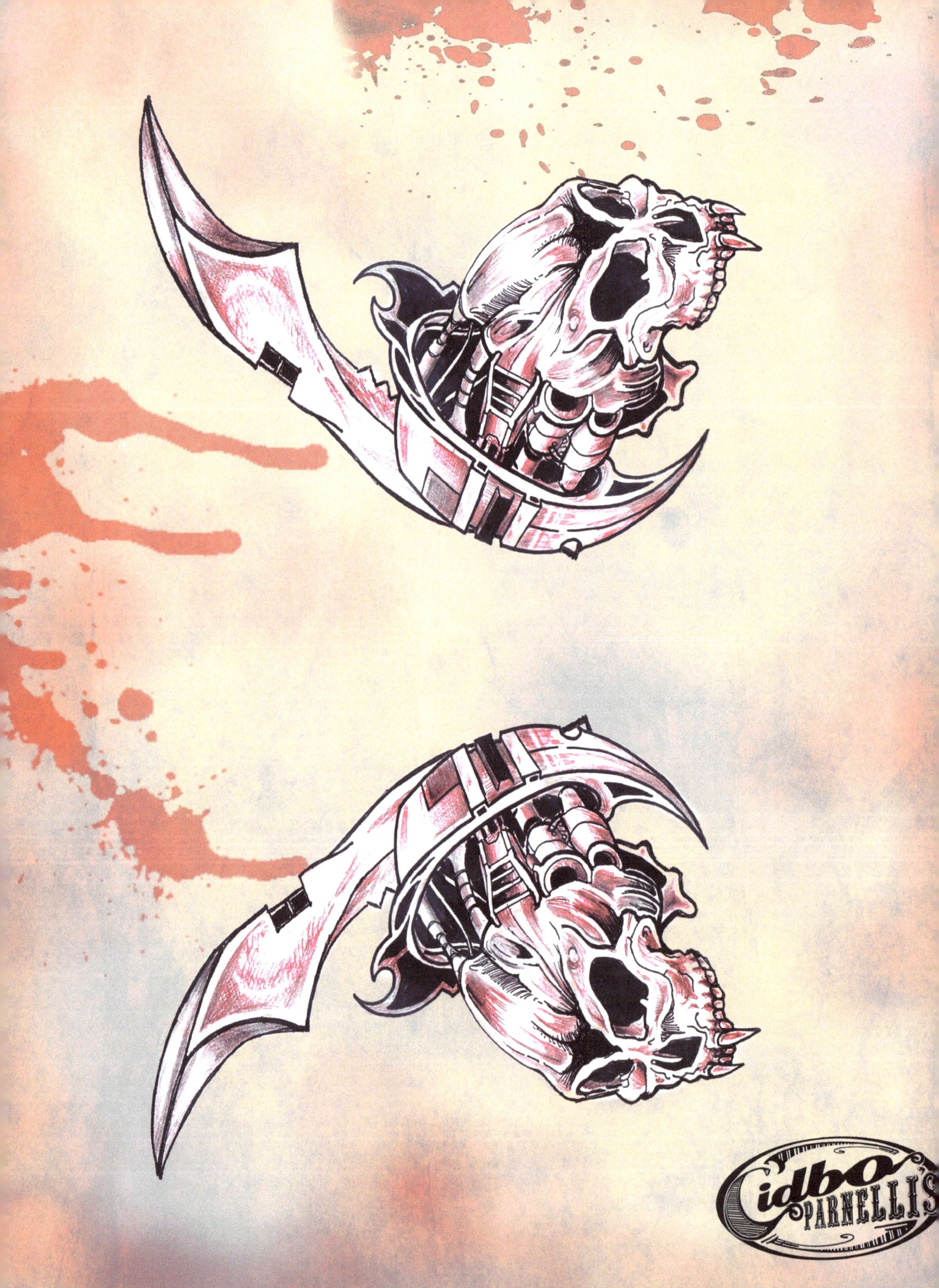

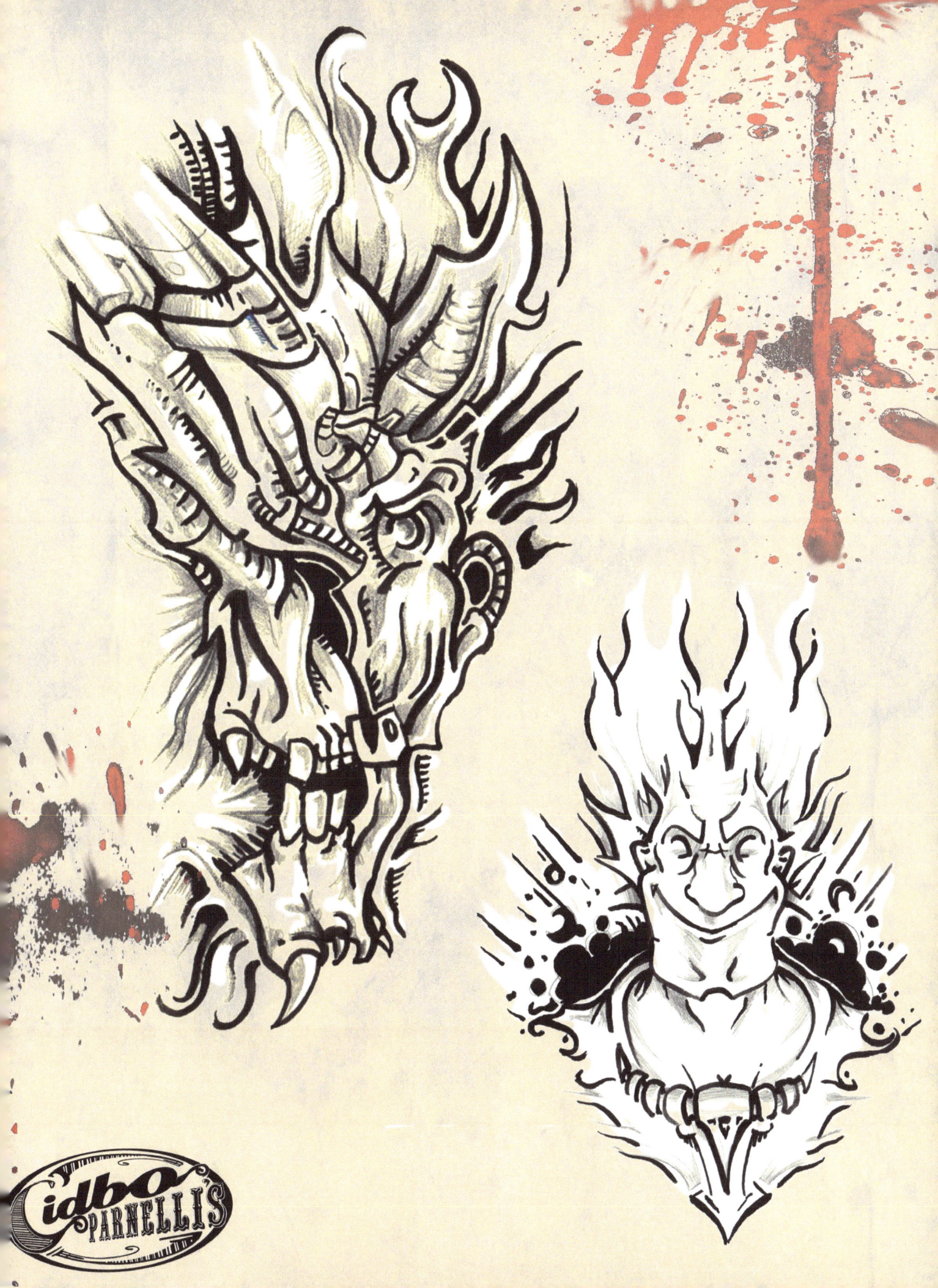

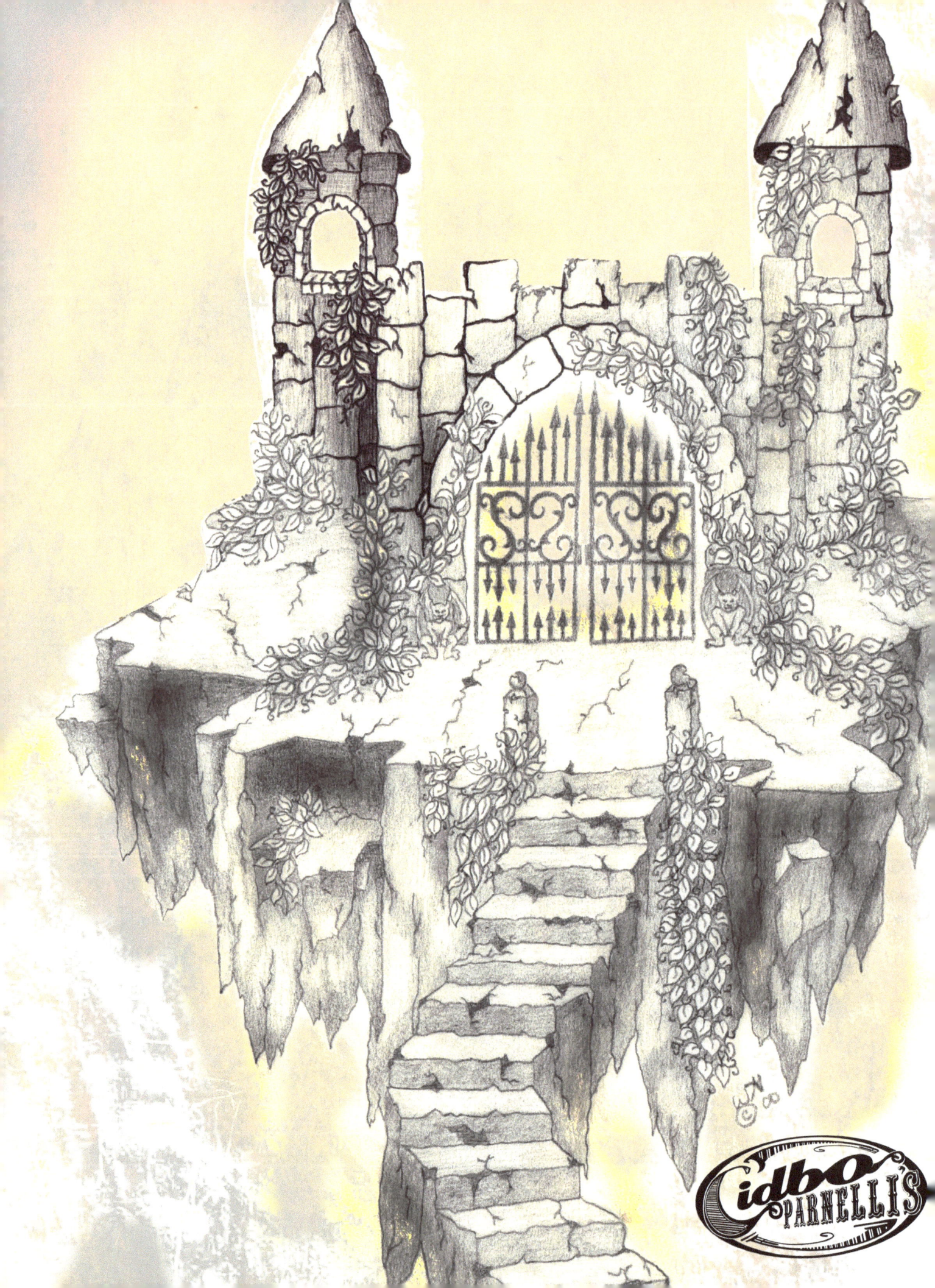

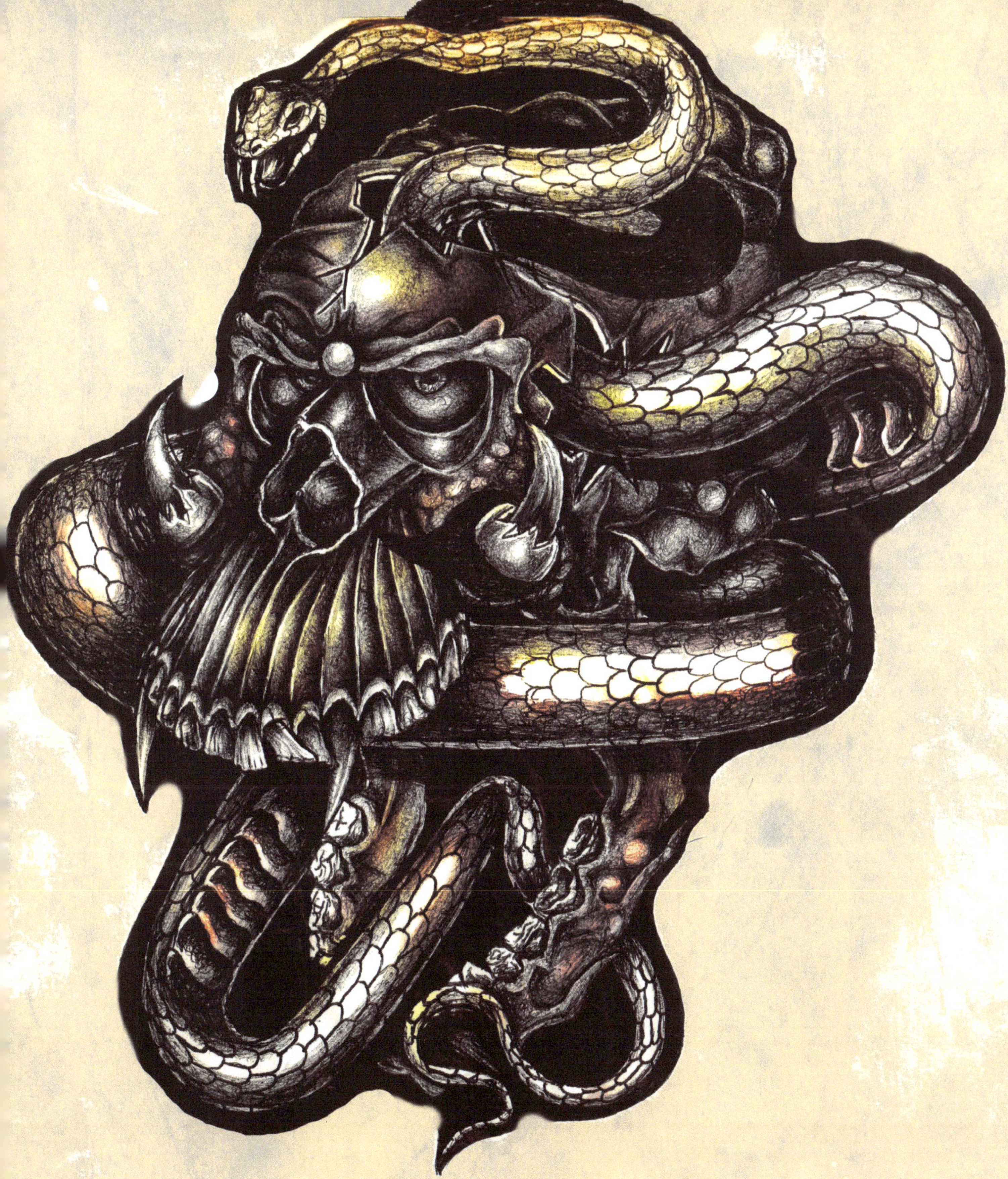

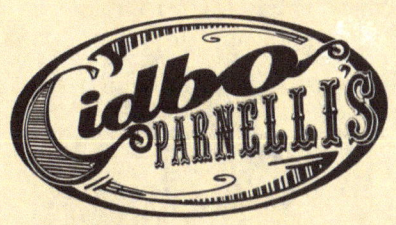

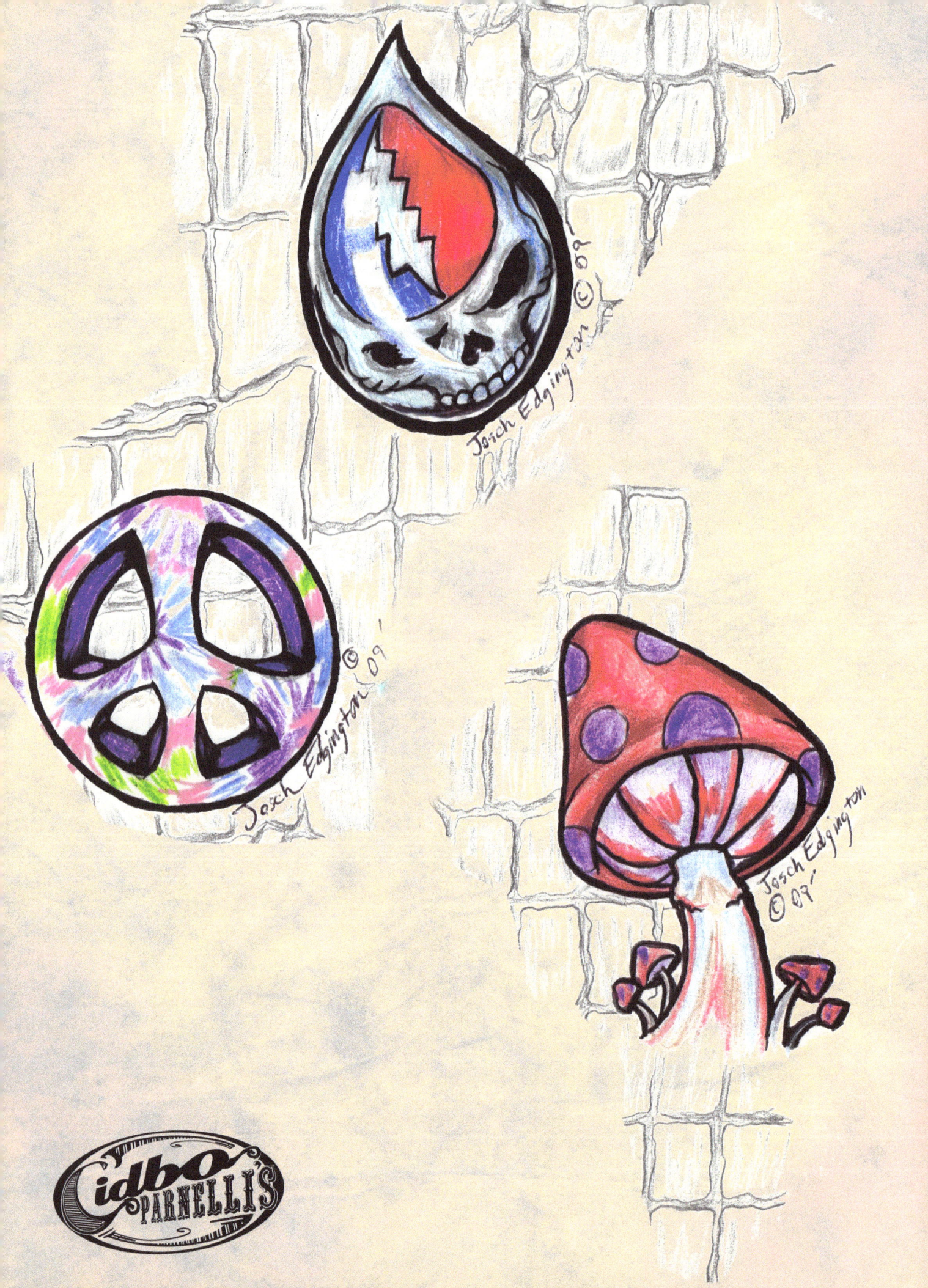

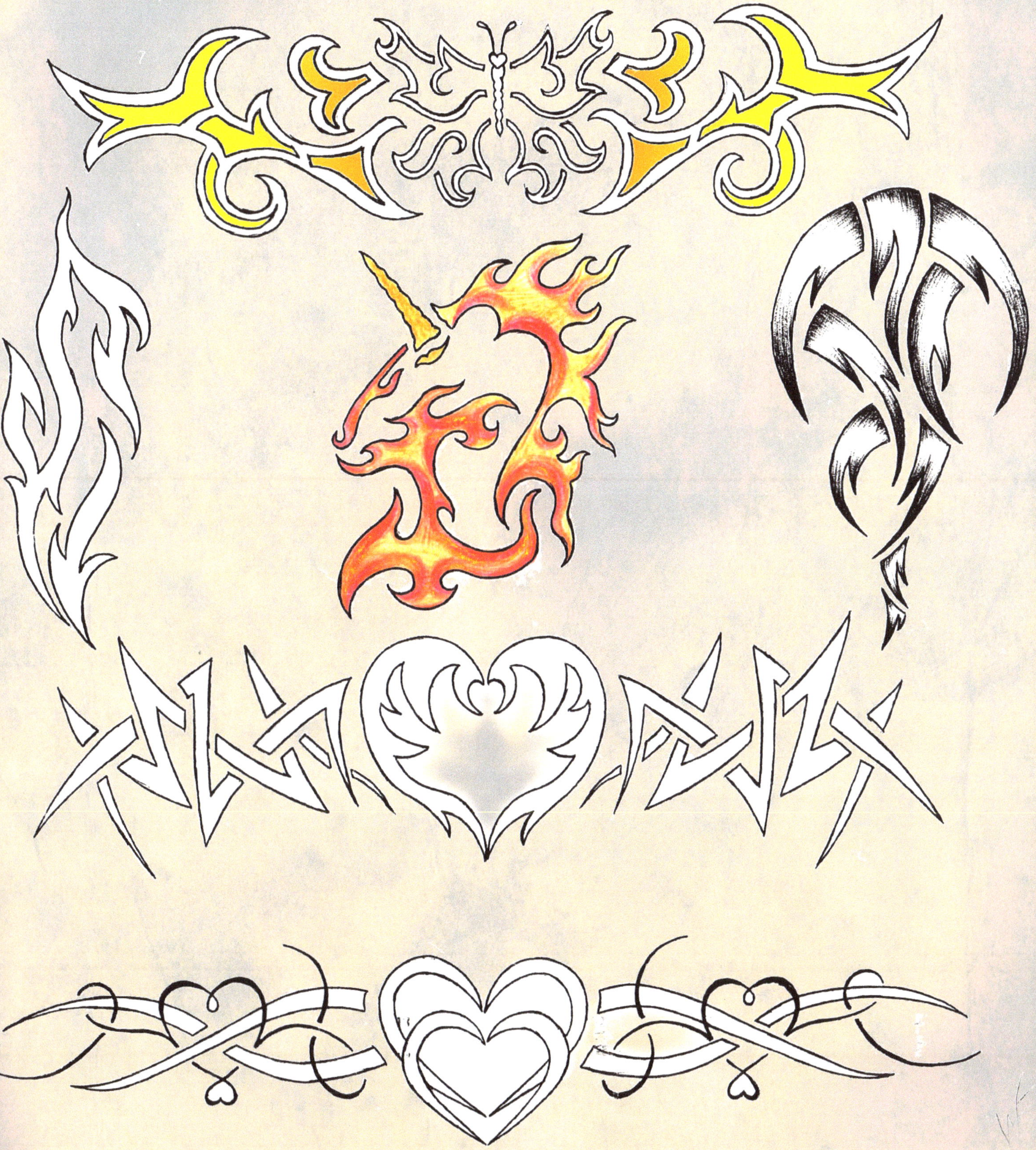

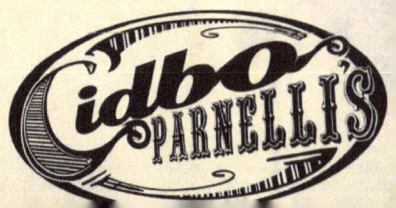

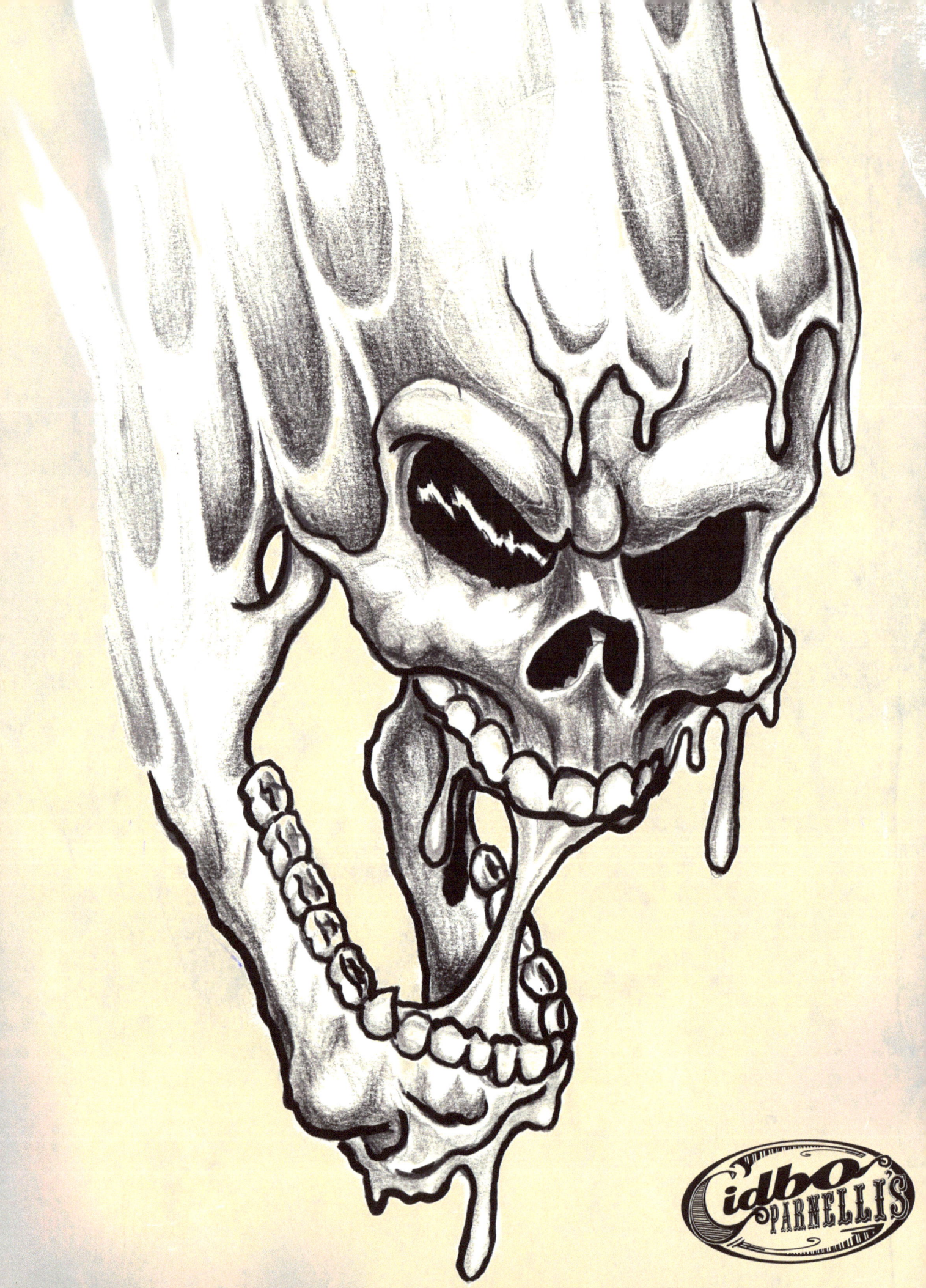

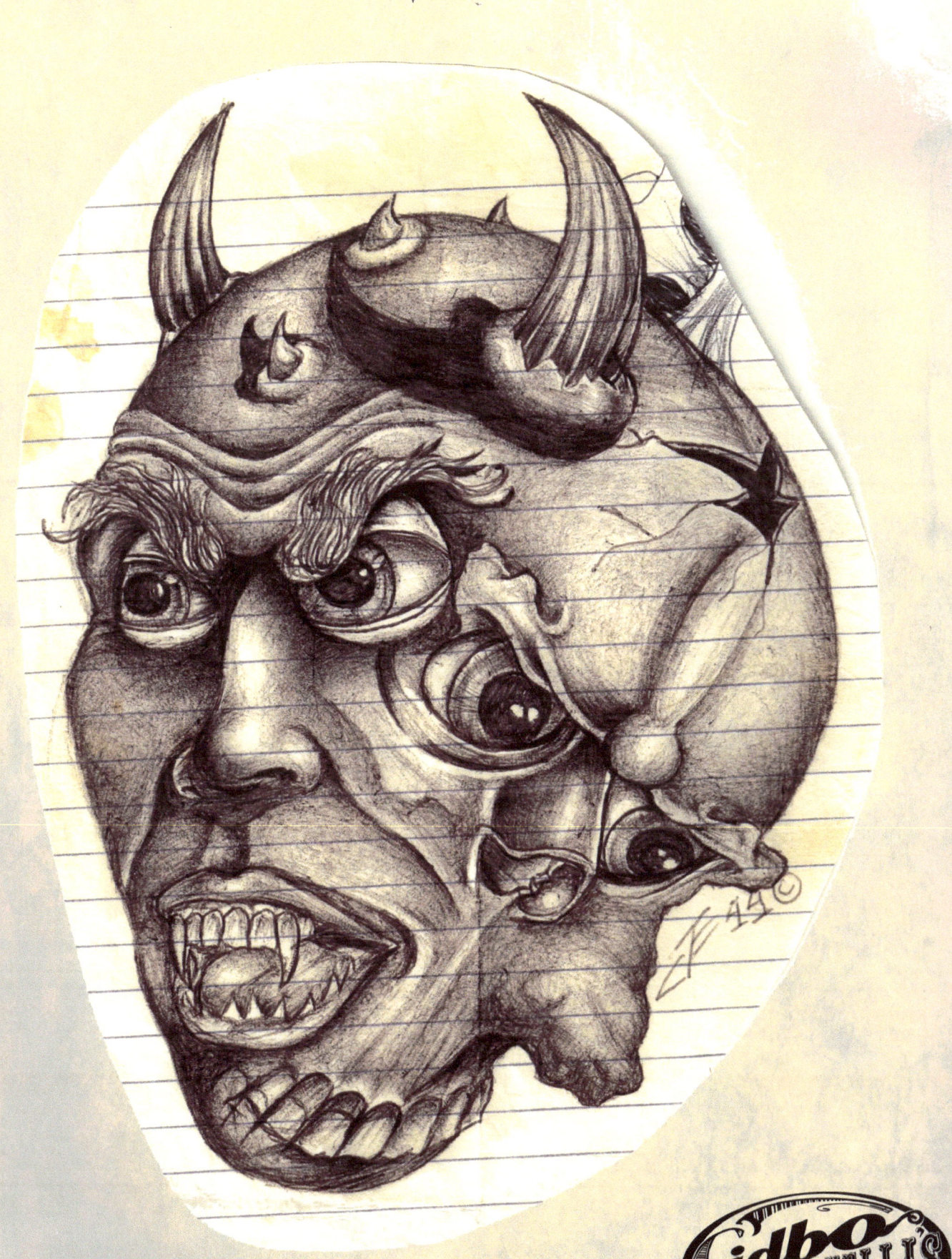

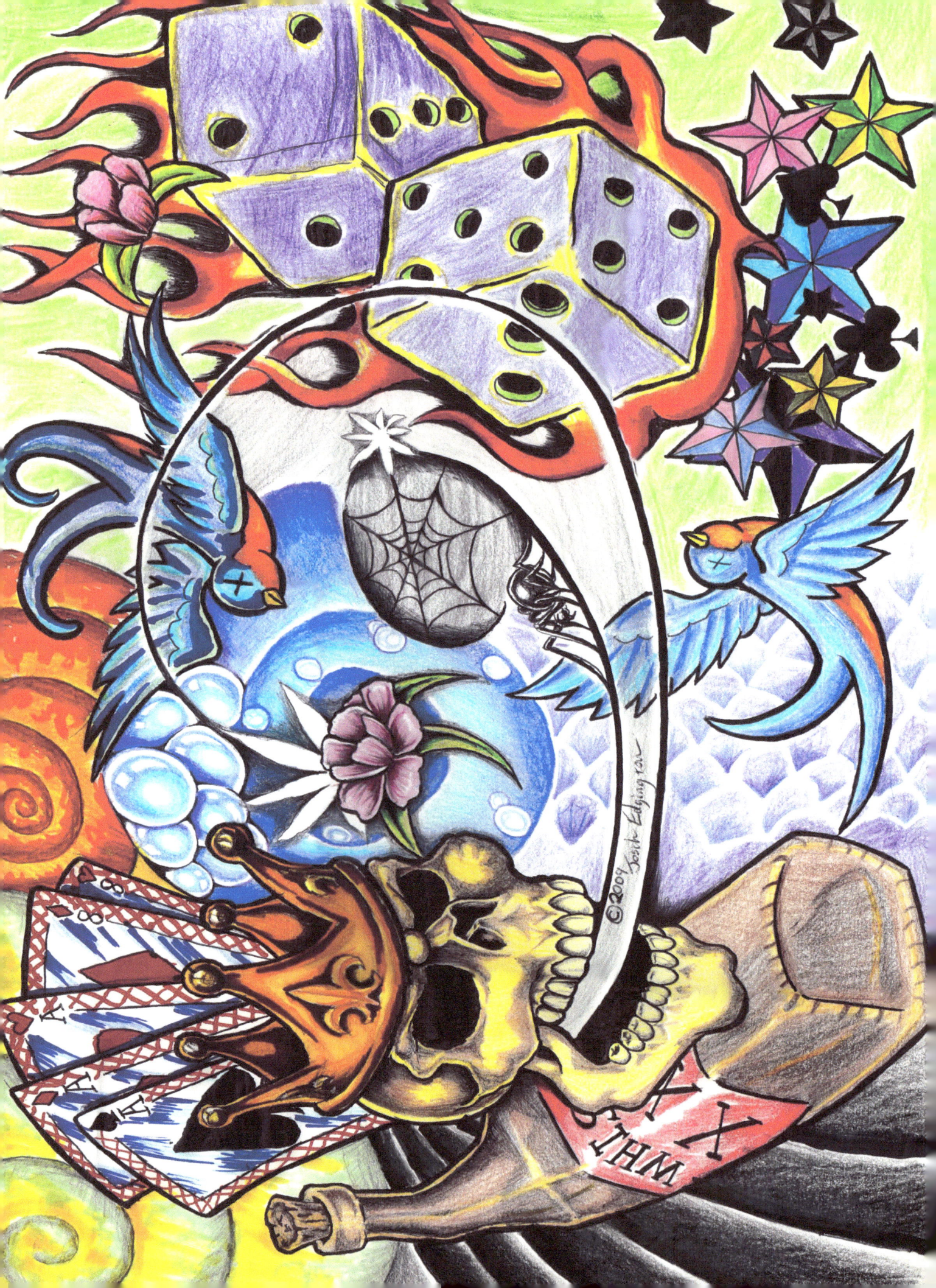

COVER DESIGN AND LAYOUT
BY
KEL LOUDERBACK
KLOUD23@GMAIL.COM

WANT A TATTOO FROM ONE OF THESE ARTIST?

CONTACT

STREET WAVES TATTOOS
1063 6TH ST., WEST PLAINS, MISSOURI 65775
(417) 256-8505

VISIT US ON THE WEB.
HTTPS://WWW.FACEBOOK.COM/CIDBOPARNELLI
HTTPS://WWW.FACEBOOK.COM/ARTWITHKEL
HTTPS://WWW.FACEBOOK.COM/STREETWAVESTATTOOS

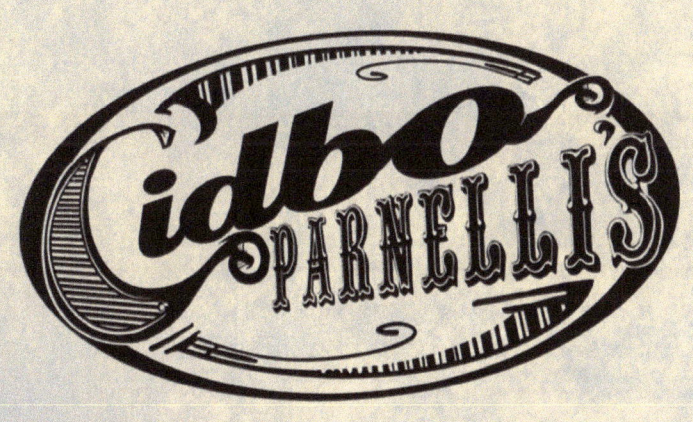

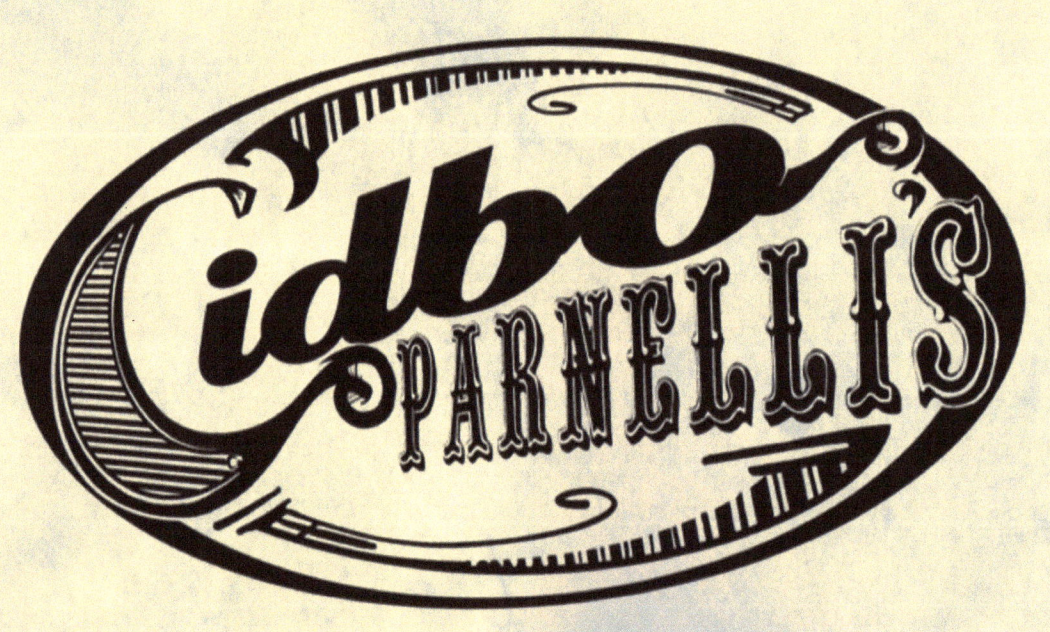